Let's Learn About Space

THE MOON

Rebecca Kraft Rector

Enslow Publishing
101 W. 23rd Street
Suite 240
New York, NY 10011
USA
enslow.com

Words to Know

atmosphere Air that surrounds a planet.

axis An imaginary line that a body turns around.

crater A hole made by the crash of a large object, such as an asteroid.

eclipse When an object is hidden by another.

gravity The force that attracts two bodies to each other.

orbit The path of an object as it circles another object in space.

rotate To turn in a circle.

satellite A man-made object that orbits an object in space.

CONTENTS

The moon orbits Earth. Some planets have no moons. Other planets have many moons.

What Is the Moon?

The moon is a rocky body. It is in space. The moon orbits Earth. It is about one-fourth the size of Earth.

FAST FACT

The moon is about 238,900 miles (384,472 kilometers) from Earth.

Earth moves around the sun. At the same time, the moon moves around Earth.

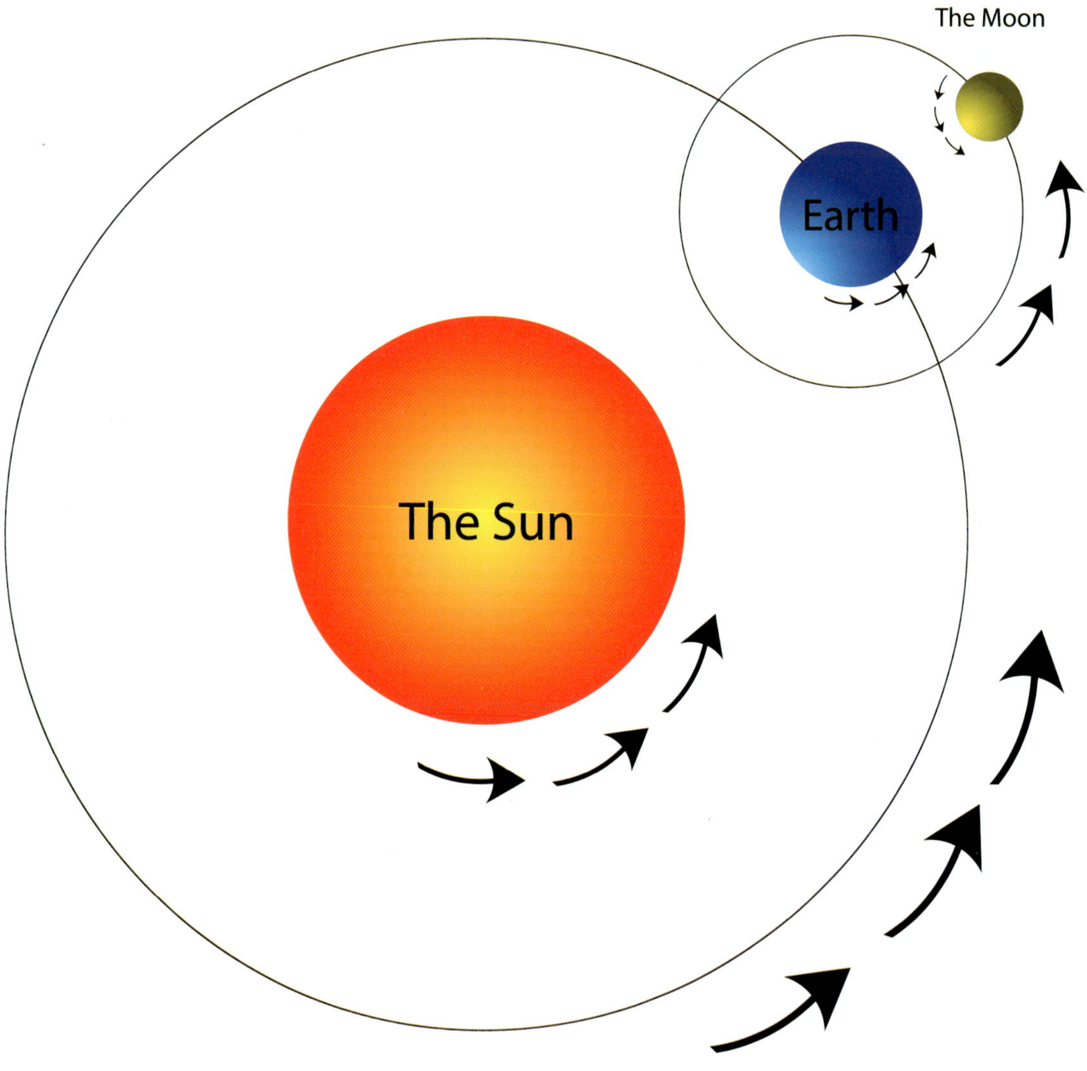

Spinning and Traveling

The moon takes about a month to travel around Earth. The moon also rotates on its axis. It takes about a month for one complete turn.

Fast Fact

Like the moon, Earth rotates on an axis.

This piece of moon rock was found in 1972, the last time men walked on the moon.

Making the Moon

Long ago, a large object struck Earth. The broken pieces formed the moon. The surface is covered by dust and rocks. The moon has mountains, craters, and valleys.

Astronauts must wear special spacesuits to help them breathe on the moon.

Atmosphere

The moon has very little atmosphere. It does not protect the moon. Meteors hit the moon and make craters. The moon does not have air that humans can breathe.

Fast Fact

There is no life on the moon.

High tides like this one
are caused by the moon.

Gravity and Tides

Gravity is weak on the moon. It is only one-sixth of Earth's gravity. The moon's gravity pulls on Earth. It moves the seas. This makes tides.

The temperature on the moon changes a lot from day to night.

Very Hot and Very Cold

The moon is very hot during the day. It can reach 260° F (127° C). It is very cold at night. It can go down to -280° F (-173° C).

A lunar eclipse happens when Earth blocks the sun's light. You can see the moon is much darker than its usual bright color.

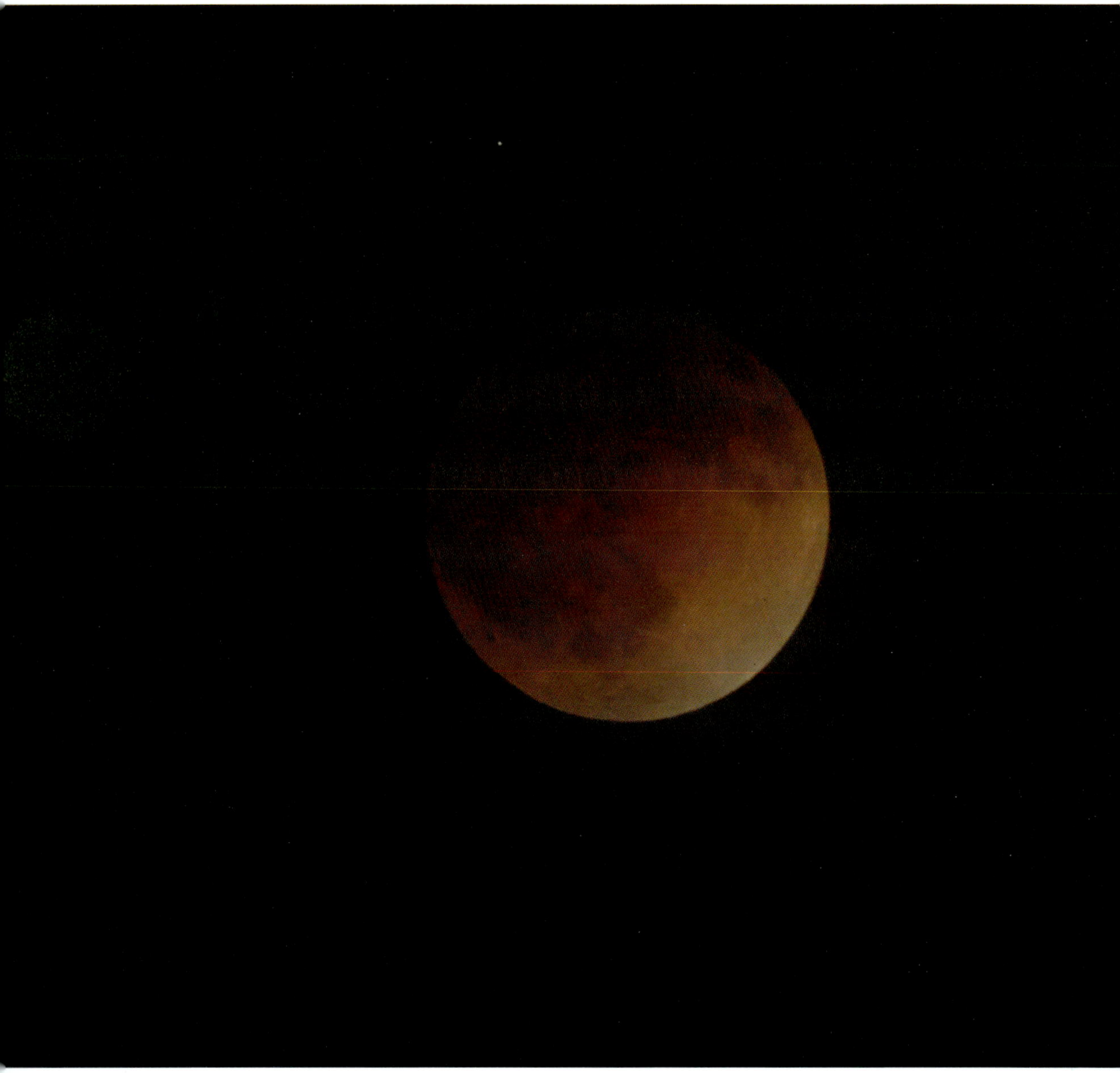

Seeing the Moon

The moon does not make its own light. It reflects the sun's light. Sometimes Earth blocks the light. It makes a shadow on the moon. This is called a lunar eclipse.

FAST FACT

The moon can sometimes be seen during the day.

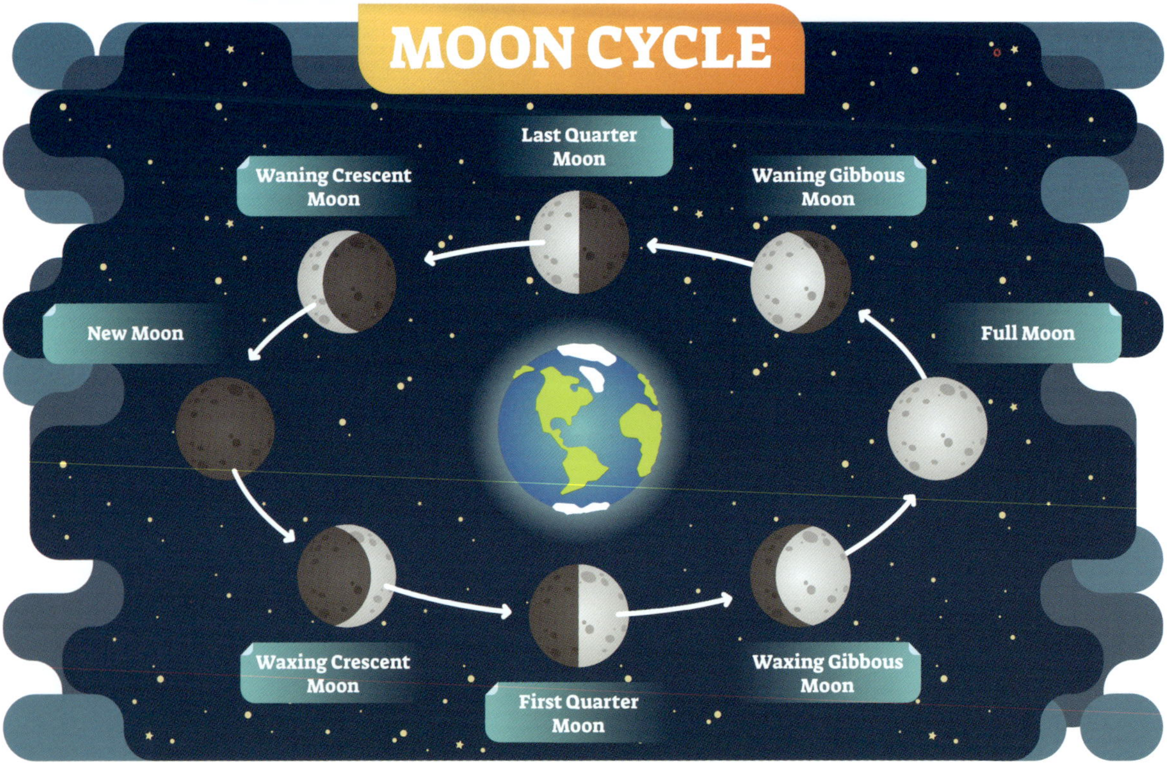

The moon goes through many phases as it orbits Earth.

Moon Shapes

People on Earth always see the same side of the moon. But that side looks different as it orbits Earth. It looks like the moon changes shape.

Fast Fact

Spacecraft show us the far side of the moon.

These footprints on the moon were left by astronauts in 1971.

Exploration

Humans study the moon. Scientists watch through telescopes. Satellites and computers find information. Spacecraft explore the moon. They also take humans there. Twelve people have walked on the moon.

FAST FACT

Neil Armstrong was the first person to walk on the moon, in 1969.

Activity

The Changing Moon

It's easy to understand the moon's changing shapes!

You are the planet Earth. The basketball is the moon. The lamp is the sun.

Materials

- A dark room
- A lamp without a shade
- A basketball

Let's get started!

Step 1: Stand several feet from the lamp. Face the light.

Step 2: Hold the ball in front of you at arm's length. The ball looks dark to you. This is the new moon.

Step 3: Turn to the left. Do not step

forward or backward. Do not twist the ball. Now the right edge of the ball is lit. This is the waxing crescent moon.

Step 4. Continue turning slowly. You will see your ball go through all the phases of the moon!

When the "moon" moves, you can see its different phases.

Learn More

Books

Branley, Franklyn M. *The Moon Seems to Change*. New York, NY: HarperCollins Children's, 2015.

DeCristofano, Carolyn Cinami. *The Sun and the Moon*. New York, NY: HarperCollins, 2016.

Hansen, Grace. *The Moon*. Minneapolis, MN: Abdo Kids, 2018.

Websites

Fly to the Moon
earthsunmoon.pingmooreandbloom.com
Explore Earth, the sun, and the moon in this fun game.

NASA: How Many Moons?
spaceplace.nasa.gov/how-many-moons/en/
Discover which planets have moons.

NASA: The Moon: Earth's Satellite
starchild.gsfc.nasa.gov/docs/StarChild/solar_system_level1/moon.html
Check out facts about the moon.

Index

Published in 2020 by Enslow Publishing, LLC.
101 W. 23rd Street, Suite 240, New York, NY 10011

Library of Congress Cataloging-in-Publication Data

Names: Rector, Rebecca Kraft, author.
Title: The moon / Rebecca Kraft Rector.
Description: New York : Enslow Publishing, 2020. |
Audience: Grade K to 4. |
Includes bibliographical references and index.
Identifiers: LCCN 2018041868| ISBN 9781978507302 (library bound) | ISBN 9781978509306 (pbk.) | ISBN 9781978509313 (6 pack) Subjects: LCSH: Moon—Juvenile literature.
Classification: LCC QB582 .R43 2019 | DDC 523.3—dc23
LC record available at https://lccn.loc.gov/2018041868

Printed in the United States of America

Photo Credits: Cover, p. 1 rangizzz/Shutterstock.com; p. 4 Baranov E/Shutterstock.com; p. 6 Nasky/Shutterstock .com; p. 8 The Natural History Museum, London/ Science Source; p. 10 Bettmann/Getty Images; p. 12 Tony Krijpipudh/Shutterstock.com; p. 14 rallef/Shutterstock .com; p. 16 NASA Ames Research Center/Brian Day; p. 18 VectorMine/Shutterstock.com; p. 20 NASA/Corbis Historical/Getty Images; p. 23 NASA/Caltech; interior design elements (planets) Vectomart/Shutterstock.com, (sun) Kirill Kirsanov/Shutterstock.com.